From Calabrian Roots to Silicon Fruit

A memoir of southern Italy's beauty, struggle and a departure

Dedication

To my father and mother, whose wisdom, love, and values have been the guiding lights of my journey, and to my brothers, who have been my steadfast companions and sources of inspiration. This book represents our shared roots and the unbreakable bonds of family.

Introduction

Calabria is where a pure blue sky meets a pristine sea. This is where my journey begins, bringing me all the way to the high-tech streets of Silicon Valley.

The South of Italy is a natural splendor; despite that, I grew up a simple guy with big dreams but from a small town. I was raised by humble parents whose wisdom and values (strongly Catholic) did impact my early life, transmitting the importance of working hard and perseverance.

During my childhood, I was surrounded by my four younger brothers. Yes, all boys. You can picture my home as an interesting, lively place, where I naturally assumed the role of mentor and protector of them. This environment nurtured in me that deep sense of responsibility and desire to reach beyond the comfort of my family's life.

Since childhood, I've been drawn to the world of technology — I remember days focused on taking apart my dad's TV remote. I love that world of tech coupled with problem solving. This interest, and my love for salsa dancing — two extremes but both artistic — painted a picture of a man, who, even if an enthusiast of the tech world, was enjoying life's moments. My travels, fueled by a taste of curiosity and ambition, led me to connect with diverse cultures and people, enriching my understanding of the world.

I've always believed in the power of making genuine connections and am known among friends for my friendly nature and humor. With this journey I want to share a tale about a tech enthusiast from a quaint little Italian town; a young dreamer, educated by life's simple lessons at home, who aspired to leave a mark in the fast-paced world of Silicon Valley, all while keeping the essence of his roots alive in his heart.

I cannot forget those summers, when, as a young boy, I used to explore the beaches that stretched along the Ionian Sea coastline. The sand, warm and decorated with pebbles, slipped between my toes as I ran towards the water's edge. That sensation — that fresh, salty smell of the sea! That sea — a blue that melted into the sky, with each slowly crashing wave, where I felt the essence of Calabria, the rhythm of life dictated by the tides, the eternal dance of land and sea.

Calabria's beauty was like no other. A region where the sand kissed by the sun seemed to hug the crystal-clear waters of the sea, and the sea in a harmoniously vista meeting the land. What an authentic mix! It is a paradise.

During summer, July to September, many families from the industrialized North would pack their bags, leaving the busy city life, and make their way to our region. They came to relax and immerse themselves in our southern world, a world of delicious cuisines, sunny days, and lazy afternoons under the shade of orange trees.

There was one evening in particular, as many, where I recall my family hosting a few guests from Milan — a city in the north of Italy. The kitchen table was laden with traditional dishes representing the flavors of my region: plates of antipasti with cured meats and local cheeses, bowls of handmade pasta drowned in fragrant tomato sauce, and platters of freshly caught seafood. Our guests marveled at the simple and exquisite flavors, the taste of the region's rich history and agricultural history.

Calabria has its unique attractiveness; however, I've noticed that for those born and raised in the United States, where I've spent the last decade of my life, the region often remains an enigma.

Friends I met during my travels around the world would express genuine curiosity when I mentioned my hometown, but it was a place they had never encountered on their world maps or travel brochures.

Through my travels, I came to understand that I had already experienced the best of what the world had to offer. I had wandered through busy markets in Thailand, marveled at the grandeur of European cities, and basked in the natural beauty of Brazil's rainforests and beaches. Honestly, nothing surprised me in the way my region had.

It was as though my homeland had set an impossibly high standard, spoiling any other destination for me. Instances like a time in New York City make me reflect. I was in a bar, in the heart of lower Manhattan, explaining the wonders of Calabria to a group of interesting people I met there. I spoke of the azure sea, the rolling vineyards, and the warmth of the people. Yet, as I spoke, I realized that no description could capture the essence of my homeland.

This book dives into my idea of this enchanting and complex region. I share stories of encounters with the 'Ndrangheta — a notorious and infamous criminal organization deeply rooted in Calabria, known for its influence and power in the region —, the challenges and the benefits of growing up within intricate family dynamics, and the vital decisions that helped me avoid the path of illegality, which some peers unfortunately chose. My story reflects determination, tracing a path from a small town in Southern Italy to the innovation epicenter, Silicon Valley.

Through these pages, I aim to convey to readers how life's choices shape our journeys. This is my story, and it's a collection of experiences, motivational tales, and life lessons. I share these insights in the hope of inspiring others to recognize the power of choices in forging one's path.

I often reflect on this: the courage to dream, determination to follow those dreams, and realization that where we come from doesn't dictate where we can go. This book represents the idea that our decisions and actions, more than our circumstances, define our life trajectory.

1. My family's outlook on life

In the big picture of my life history, the threads of responsibility, tradition, and love were woven together from an early age. As the eldest of five brothers, my journey through life has been colored by the unique experiences and responsibilities that come with this position.

My parents, each with their unique duties and backgrounds, played crucial roles in shaping the structure of our family life. My dad was a skilled barber with an adventurous spirit, who, before my birth, embarked on a remarkable chapter of his life in Melbourne, Australia.
My mom, a compassionate and nurturing soul, added a touch of love and warmth to every corner of our home.

This is a look into the foundation of my family and the story of my life, where tradition, artisanship, and a deep sense of family intertwined to create a rich curtain of experiences.

From a young age, I assumed the role of elder brother; of course, from birth order, but also to look out for my younger siblings. There are many of those early mornings still clear in my mind. I would help my brothers get ready for school, making sure they had their backpacks packed and their shoelaces tied. I'd patiently sit with them, offering help with homework and answering their curious questions about the world. It wasn't always easy, but I took pride in being their guide and protector.

There's one humorous memory that stands out, involving my second brother. When he was a little baby and cried relentlessly, I found a rather innovative solution to keep him calm: a pacifier dipped in honey.

This remedy miraculously transformed his tears into smiles, leaving us both laughing. The only catch was that it seemed to trigger an unexpected, shall we say, "consequence" — a ton of messy diapers.

My dad had honed his craft over the years, and his barbershop was always bursting with friends and storytelling. Dad's passion for his work was contagious, and I often found myself observing him at the barbershop, learning about the art of the straight razor shave, the importance of a well-trimmed beard and haircut done well. His dedication to his profession was matched only by his love for our family.

My father's tales of his time in Australia were like a never ending adventure book with chapters full of humor and nostalgia. One of the most vivid stories centered around his cherished possession: a red MG convertible. He loved this car to the point where it almost felt like a member of our family.

Every time he shared this story, he'd start by pulling out a worn photo album. The photos were faded but held an attraction that transcended time. As he turned the pages, his eyes would light up, and he'd launch into a detailed narrative.

He'd tell me about the sensation of freedom he experienced while driving that MG along the coastal roads of Australia. His description of the wind tousling his hair and the exhilarating roar of the engine made me feel like I was right there with him. According to Dad, that car had a personality of its own, and he'd joke that it often had a mind of its own too.

One story in particular, he loved to recount. He'd describe a day when he decided to take the MG for a spin along the stunning Great Ocean Road. As he cruised alongside the rugged cliffs, a seagull apparently mistook his car for a gigantic piece of bread. With a hearty laugh, Dad would mime the seagull's dive-bombing antics and how he had to dodge avian kamikaze attacks while trying to enjoy his scenic drive.

And through every recounting of this tale, we'd share laughs, and I'd feel a connection to a time and place I had never experienced. Dad's stories had a way of making the past come alive, and that red MG became a legendary character in our family.

It was during his time in Melbourne that Dad's sense of humor, already infectious, reached new heights. He brought back with him a distinct Aussie accent and a repertoire of jokes that would keep us laughing for years. Melbourne had been a fantastic chapter in his life and become part of our family's heritage, to consider as our first connection to a world beyond our small sea town.

After two decades of life in Melbourne, a twist of fate brought my dad back to our hometown, setting the stage for a romance that seemed almost predestined. It was there he met my mom; their paths intersected in a beautiful narrative of serendipity.

My mom, the third of four siblings, brought compassionate energy to our home. She was the heart of our family, creating an environment filled with warmth and affection. Mom's talents as a hairdresser extended far beyond her salon: She used her skills to bring comfort and dignity to the elderly in our community. Her hearted nature left an indelible mark on all who knew her.

Mom had an incredibly kind soul; a central figure in our family. Her intelligence shone brightly, even though she didn't pursue formal education beyond high school. It was something I often wondered about

— why she didn't continue her studies — especially considering her passion for learning.

One of my most lovely memories is of sitting with her as she thumbed through a box of her childhood belongings. She pulled out old notebooks and faded homework assignments from her school days, her eyes lighting up with enthusiasm. It were as if these relics transported her back to a time when she was a young student full of dreams and aspirations.

She shared these notions of her past with me and explained the subjects she had excelled in and the teachers who had recognized her potential. Her descriptions were so vivid that I could almost picture her as a diligent student, eager to absorb knowledge. It was evident that she had an incredible love for learning, and her childhood achievements were demonstrating her intelligence.

Despite all that, life had taken her on a different path; one that led to a successful career as a hairdresser. She became renowned in our town for her skill, transforming ordinary hair into works of art and boosting the confidence of her clients. People often spoke of her warmhearted nature and how she made every visit to the salon feel like a visit with a dear friend.

In many ways, my mother's story shows how the paths we choose in life are often shaped by a multitude of factors, including the opportunities available to us and the roles we assume within our families. Her decision to become a hairdresser didn't diminish her intellect or passion for learning; instead, it showed her adaptability and the depth of her character.

As I think about her life and her support for my own educational journey, I realize that her influence extended far beyond her career. She instilled in me a love for knowledge and a drive to pursue my studies. She gave me a gift; one that would change my future in profound ways.

The union of my parents created the family life I was born into — a life rich with tradition, brimming with laughter, and deeply founded in the values they cherished. Growing up in such a nurturing environment, I was constantly enveloped in warmth and love, which profoundly impacted my emotional development.

From the joyous celebrations to the quiet moments of understanding, each aspect contributed to a strong sense of belonging and identity. This environment I was surrounded by on a daily basis allowed me to develop a deep emotional intelligence, an understanding and appreciation for the variability of relationships and human connections. I learned the importance of empathy, the strength that comes from vulnerability, and the strong bonds of family — unbreakable.

These experiences made me feel loved and supported, providing a foundation of stability and confidence. They taught me the value of close relationships and the profound impact of a supportive family.

As I grew and ventured into the world, these lessons and emotions stayed with me, guiding my interactions and shaping my approach to life's challenges and opportunities. My family's influence was the compass that helped me navigate through life, always pointing me back to the values and love that defined my growth.

So, what exactly did I learn? Well, from my dad, I learned the art of resilience and the importance of adaptability. His journey back from Melbourne to our hometown taught me that life is a series of flows, and it's our ability to navigate these changes that defines us.

From Mom, with her passion for hairdressing and deep love for family, I absorbed the significance of pursuing one's passions and the value of nurturing close family ties.

Growing up next to my siblings, I was constantly learning — from the joys of shared experiences to the challenges of resolving disagreements. Being the oldest, I quickly learned the responsibility that comes with leadership and the importance of setting a positive example. We all learned the art of compromise and mutual support.

Over time, these family experiences transformed my character and choices. The lessons of resilience, passion, leadership, and empathy have been cornerstones in my personal and professional life. These key fundamentals influenced my approach to challenges, my ambitions, and my interactions with others. In essence, my family was my first school, and the lessons learned within its walls navigated me in the wider world.

Now, as we dive into the roots of Calabria, that lovely region and cherished land, we'll explore how these values and my family would shape my journey through life in this timeless southern Italian region.

2. Roots in Calabria

The date of my birth was etched in the memory of my entire family. With many others in this region. It was here, in the heart of South Italy, that I came into the world on a warm November morning in 1986, in this land as timeless as the Ionian Sea, Calabria.

The Calabrian population treasure their origins and celebrate them with fervor; whether through the annual 'Nduja festival, Tarantella music, or simply the joy of sharing a meal with loved ones under the shade of an orange tree.

We Calabrians are called *Terroni*, a term lovingly coined by our Northern compatriots meaning "workers of the land," due to our resilience and unbreakable connection to the earth. The land, bountiful and unforgiving, had shaped our character, and I believe this ingredient instilled in us a deep appreciation for all that it provided.

Hot summer afternoons aren't rare. I would wander the groves of orange trees that filled the hillsides. The fruit, golden and radiant, hung like ornaments from the branches. I'd pluck one, the scent of citrus filling the air, and share it with my brothers.

We'd race each other to the rocky cliffs that overlooked the azure sea, the waves crashing against the ancient rocks below. In those moments, we embodied the spirit of the Terroni, working the land, savoring its fruits, and reveling in the beauty that surrounded us.

Calabria, my beloved homeland, was a way of life, a heritage to be loved, and a foundation upon which I would build my future. As I grew, I began to understand that the lessons learned by the sides of my wise parents would shape my journey in ways I could scarcely imagine.

The economy was often as capricious as the winter sea. Many families had watched their sons and daughters leave for the industrialized North, chasing dreams of steady employment. Yet, Calabrians managed their finances with wisdom, for they knew the value of every hard-earned euro. Frugality was a virtue passed down through generations, and even in times of plenty, the lessons of thriftiness were never forgotten.

One evening, I sat with my grandmother on the sun-warmed steps of our family's old stone house. The scent of basil and tomatoes wafted from her kitchen as she crafted pasta from scratch. She shared stories of her own youth, when our regional economy was even tougher. She recalled how her family relied on the land and knew the taste of every fruit, every vegetable, every olive they harvested.

With nostalgia in her eyes, she spoke of a time when neighbors traded goods, when a simple meal was a feast, and when laughter under the stars was the only entertainment needed. "We might not have had much," she said, "but we had each other, and we had Calabria.

As a child, I used to accompany my parents to the family's olive grove. The silver-green trees stood like ancient sentinels, their roots delving deep into the rich Calabrian soil. My dad, Franco, or Papà, a weathered man with hands as calloused as the sand along the coast, taught me the art of cultivating olives. He would say, "These trees, they are our roots, the lifeblood of our land." With a knowing smile, he would tell tales of generations past, how our ancestors toiled on this very land, and how people far beyond the region sought our family's olive oil.

I remember the fantastic days of my childhood in Calabria, where every season brought its own rhythm to our lives. It was a place where the land was as much part of our family as any of us, and Papà was its dedicated custodian.

In the spring, Papà would gather us, his five sons, to plant tomatoes. He had learned the ritual process from his father and passed it down to us. With dirt-stained hands and sun-kissed faces, we'd follow him to the family's plot of land.

The land had been in our family for probably three generations, and its rich, dark soil was the lifeblood of our home. Papà would mark rows in the earth, each perfectly spaced. We'd kneel in the soil, digging small holes for the tomato seedlings. As the sun beat down on us, Papà's hands would cradle each fragile plant, guiding it into the earth.

As the seasons shifted, so did our duties. The olive trees that dotted the landscape demanded our attention. Collecting olives was a very arduous task, one that required substantial patience and persistence.

Of course, without the aid of modern technology, we relied on our hands and simple tools. Each morning, at the first light of dawn, we'd make our way to the grove. My brothers and I would spread large, weathered sheets beneath the trees, forming a canvas to catch the falling olives.

With practiced precision, Papà would take a long stick and gently tap the branches, coaxing the olives to rain down upon us. The rhythmic thud of the stick echoed through the grove as the precious fruit fell, landing with soft thumps on the sheets below.

One particular late autumn evening, the olives needed to be collected urgently. A big looming storm threatened to damage the crop. Under a moonlit sky, we gathered beneath the olive trees, our lanterns casting flickering shadows. The scent of the olive grove mingled with the crisp night air. We worked in near silence, the only sounds the rustling of leaves, the olives in baskets, and the occasional laughter that erupted when a rogue olive struck someone's head.

Papà was also quick to anger when he discovered that animals, particularly cows, had destroyed the boundaries he had meticulously crafted of wood and iron. The sight of those boundaries in disarray would ignite a fiery determination within him to restore order and maintain the integrity of our land.

Our family's land was a treasure trove of agricultural abundance, offering olives, oranges, tomatoes, and vineyards heavy with plump grapes. These vineyards held the promise of sweet nectar, and every year, our family eagerly awaited the grape harvest.

As summer transitioned into autumn, the grapes reached peak ripeness. The land came alive with activity, a buzzing energy that signaled the time had come to gather nature's bounty.

We'd gather in the crisp morning air, baskets in hand, ready for the labor-intensive but rewarding task of grape harvesting. Each vine held clusters of grapes, glistening with dew and kissed by the golden rays of the sun. We'd carefully cut these clusters, ensuring that only the juiciest grapes made it into our baskets.

Once the baskets were filled to the brim, we'd transport our grape treasures to a central location on the property. Here, we'd set up makeshift tables, and the real magic of winemaking would begin. We destemmed and sorted the grapes, separating them from any debris.

Then came the thrilling part — the grapes were squeezed by my dad's hand-powered machine, *il torchio*, the press. This device, with its wooden and metal components, allowed us to extract the juice with precision and care.

As we turned the wheel and the press exerted gentle pressure on the grapes, juice would flow, releasing the rich, fruity aroma that signaled the birth of our wine.

This freshly pressed juice, known as *mosto* (must) , was collected in barrels, and the process of fermentation began. Our family's winemaking traditions were cherished. We'd allow the must to ferment naturally, with yeast from the grape skins, in large wooden barrels. The transformation from sweet juice to robust wine was a slow and patient one, overseen by generations of winemakers.

As the weeks passed, the must would bubble and hiss, filling the air with gasses and fragrances. We'd check its progress, tasting the evolving flavors and waiting for just the right moment to transfer the wine into storage barrels.

These barrels, made of chestnut, were like time capsules. They'd cradle the wine for months, sometimes years, allowing it to mature and develop its character. Our wine, more than a beverage, was a living vibe to our connection with the land, and to the rich traditions of Calabria.

When the time was finally right, we'd gather once more, this time to bottle our wine. Each bottle was filled with care, sealed with a cork, and labeled. These bottles would find their place in our family cellar, where they'd rest and age, awaiting special occasions and celebrations.

The process of grape harvesting and winemaking was a labor of love and a cue that the fruits of our labor would bring joy to our family for years to come.

And when the wine was finally ready to drink, and my dad uncorked a bottle, it was like he was unveiling the Holy Grail of Elixir, a potion so pure and natural that even Mother Nature took notes. He'd raise the glass in a toast to his vineyard adventures and say, "Folks, what we have here is better than medicine. It's the elixir that keeps doctors jealous and grapes blushing." We'd all laugh, knowing that this wine was indeed a remedy for the soul and a reward for his winemaking prowess.

These rich experiences strongly impacted my aspirations, values, and beliefs.

Working alongside my father and brothers in the fields, tending to olives and grapes, instilled in me a deep appreciation for the art of cultivation, both of the land and of one's character.

The process of planting, nurturing, and harvesting was a powerful metaphor for life and taught me patience, resilience, and the importance of careful attention to detail. I learned that dedication and passion could turn simple fruits of labor into something extraordinary, much like how one's efforts in life can yield remarkable results.

These early lessons in agriculture mirrored the values I would carry forward: the belief in hard work, the importance of family unity in achieving common goals, and a respect for the natural world.

My father's humor and joy in winemaking, his reverence for tradition, and his ability to turn every task into an adventure had an enormous influence on my outlook.

I grew to understand that life, much like winemaking, is a blend of science and art, of tradition and innovation.

Reaching our family's land was no easy feat. It was nestled twenty minutes from our home, accessible only through a network of dirt roads forgotten by time. The journey was an adventure in itself.

The roads were rough and pitted with potholes, a treacherous path for our aging car. Yet, Papà navigated them with skill honed over the years. He knew every bend and bump, every hidden pitfall. With a practiced hand on the wheel, he guided us through the darkness, avoiding the treacherous potholes that lurked like traps in the moonlight.

We embarked on these journeys from the property and back in Papà's possession, a 1972 Fiat 500, a car that held a special place in his heart. The little white car had seen countless trips to our family's land, carrying not just us but generations of memories.

This compact car had seen it all, from bumpy rides on dirt roads to hauling sacks of tomatoes and crates of olives. It was practically an extension of our family, bearing the marks of countless journeys to the property and back.

Papà had owned that Fiat 500 for years, and he put it through its paces. The little car chugged along faithfully, despite the wear and tear it suffered on our agricultural adventures. It became a symbol of resilience, like our family's enduring connection to the land.

But, as you can imagine, years of rough handling took its toll on the poor Fiat. It was showing its age. That's when Papà made a decision that would later become a source of endless laughter in our family.

He decided to sell the Fiat 500 to our cousin for a modest sum. My cousin, also a car enthusiast, saw the potential in the little car. He took it upon himself to restore it to its former glory. With meticulous care and a lot of elbow grease, my cousin worked wonders on the Fiat.

The Fiat 500, now looking pristine and well maintained, was ready to hit the road once more. But just as my cousin was enjoying the fruits of his labor, fate intervened in the form of my youngest brother's arrival.

Papà needed the Fiat 500 again, this time for Mamma, who required a car with the new addition to the family. Without hesitation, Papà reclaimed the car he had sold to my cousin, with a sheepish grin that seemed to say, "I guess I'll be needing this back."

To add a comical twist to the story, Papà never actually paid my cousin for the restoration work he had done. It became a running joke in the family, with Papà playfully avoiding the subject whenever it came up. That Fiat 500 was absolutely a representation of our adventures to our land, the quirks and humor that made our family so unique.

3. The multicolored flavors of Calabria

Within the walls of our family's house is where I first learned to appreciate the culinary wonders of this region, where sea abundance and earth richness melt together, and where flavors are the incarnation of love and tradition, not just the taste palate. Yes, I was raised with a strong and genuine food culture.

Summer was the season of magic. The fragrant air filled with a unique fresh and salty sea smell that always awoke memories of adventures with family and friends. It was during these summer vacations that I would gather with my four brothers — Daniele, Stefano, Andrea, and the youngest, Lorenzo, who spread energy from his every pore — to cook seafood dishes like *pasta allo scoglio*.

Under the eye of my parents, me, Stefano, Andrea, and Lorenzo would prepare the ingredients in our kitchen with laughter and friendly banter. Meanwhile, Daniele, our videographer extraordinaire, captured every moment of our culinary adventures.

His video blogs would later become a cherished family archive, proving our shared love for cooking and capturing the best moments.

Creating pasta allo scoglio began with Lorenzo making a trip to the local seafood market, where we could always find the freshest fish, in the morning when he'd select the catch of the day. Shrimp, mussels, clams, and tender calamari became the stars of our culinary canvas.

Back in our family kitchen, my brothers and I would gather around the table, each of us assigned a specific task. Stefano was the master of deveining shrimp, his fingers swift and deft as he removed the digestive tract. Andrea meticulously cleaned and scrubbed the mussels, banishing their sandy grit.

I was assigned to prepare the seafood cream that would infuse our dish with the essence of the sea. In a large pan, we'd sauté garlic and red chili pepper flakes in olive oil until they released their tantalizing aroma.

As the seafood sizzled and released its essence, the cream took shape, carrying the expected promise of a dish that would transport us to the shores of the Ionian Sea. The sauce that would hug our pasta was a symphony of sea flavors, a taste that sticks in your mind for years.

Mamma, a culinary maestro in her own right, had her specialty: *risotto ai funghi porcini* (risotto with porcini mushrooms). The aroma of the forest seemed to waft from the pot as she carefully stirred arborio rice, wild porcini mushrooms handpicked by Papà, and a dash of white wine. Each bite was a journey into the woods, a taste of Calabria's pristine landscapes.

Then, Papà, whose culinary prowess extended to the savory *pasta alla Corte d'Assise*. The dish's name, with its complex flavors, was a nod to the courthouse and it combined pasta, tomato sauce, parsley, and a medley of local spices. Papà passed down the secret recipe for this rustic masterpiece through generations.

The final act was a harmonious blend of our efforts. The pasta, al dente and brimming with anticipation, was tossed into the pan with the seafood. Mamma's risotto would nestle alongside Papà's pasta alla Corte d'Assise.

Nonna, the matriarch of our family, would spend hours in the kitchen, the wooden table covered in a multitude of ingredients. Her lasagna was a delicacy, the essence of passion that combined handmade pasta sheets, layers of provola cheese, *prosciutto cotto* (cured ham), and the most flavorful tomato-meat sauce you can imagine.

As she assembled the dishes, Nonna would tell us stories of generations past, of how her own grandmother had taught her the secrets of pasta making, to ensure that tradition flowed through the family like a river.

While Daniele's role as our family videographer, capturing these moments, reinforced the value of documenting our shared experiences, turning simple meals into memories, the table was set. With all the culinary creations ready, the family would gather. Believe me, each bite was a journey through Calabria's flavors.

Though Papà has passed away, Mamma and Nonna were still very much part of our lives. I would visit them two or three times a year, returning to the place where my love for food, family, and tradition were nurtured. Despite the passage of time and the changing seasons, the flavors of the South of Italy and the warmth of family will forever remain a cherished part of my life.

These experiences gave me invaluable lessons of collaboration, tradition, and the importance of preserving family heritage. Cooking with my parents and my brothers was a dance of unity, teaching us the art of working together harmoniously.

All this profoundly shaped my values and aspirations. It taught me the significance of maintaining cultural traditions, the joy of creating something beautiful from simple ingredients, and the importance of family bonds.

I understood the simplest acts, when done with love and care, can leave the most lasting impressions. In every endeavor, I carry with me the multicolored flavors of my childhood, the warmth of family gatherings, and the belief that in bringing people together, we can create something extraordinary.

4. Festa di San Rocco (Feast of Saint Rocco)

One weekend each year, my hometown comes alive with an energy and spirit unlike any other. It's a commemoration that we eagerly await, a tradition ingrained in the heart of our community. The Festa di San Rocco is a time-honored event that captivates every sense and fills the heart with reverence and joy.

As the days draw nearer to this grand occasion, a palpable excitement envelops the town. Streets that are usually serene and tranquil buzz with activity. Preparations for the festival are meticulous and thorough, as if the entire town holds its breath in anticipation.

The festivities kick off with a religious procession, a display of devotion and tradition. The statue of San Rocco, draped in rich vestments, is carried through the streets on the shoulders of the devoted. The air is filled with the hauntingly beautiful melodies of the local band, their sad yet inspiring notes providing a backdrop to this sacred journey.

Well, it's not all solemnity. The streets turn into a lively marketplace, with stalls offering an array of local delicacies, artisanal crafts, and souvenirs.

The Calabrian cuisine takes center stage, with fragrant pasta sauces simmering, golden arancini beckoning, and the irresistible aroma of *panino con salsiccia* (artisanal sausage inside panini bread) floating through the air.

The culmination of each day's festivities is a magnificent fireworks display that lights up the night sky in a breathtaking spectacle. It's a fitting tribute to the festival's vibrancy and the unity of our community.

For the people of our town, the Festa di San Rocco is an annual reaffirmation of their shared history and values. It's a time to come together, to strengthen bonds, and to renew their faith in those enduring traditions that connect them to their ancestors and the rich cultural heritage they proudly uphold.

In the middle of the lively streets surrounded by colorful banners and echoing with the sounds of the tarantella dance (our traditional folk dance), the *bancarelle* emerges as a vibrant component of the Festa di San Rocco. These market stalls, often arranged in rows that seem to stretch endlessly, are a treasure trove of goods and delicacies that add to the festive atmosphere.

Many of the bancarelle observe the region's culinary excellence. Here, you can discover an array of local specialties, from freshly harvested produce to homemade jams and preserves. Stalls are lined with plump, sun-ripened tomatoes, glistening eggplants, and bundles of fresh basil — the essential ingredients for creating the region's iconic dishes.

I recall, anytime I walked the streets, being tantalized by the aroma of roasted peppers and onions sizzling on large grills. These vegetables are transformed into *peperonata*, a sweet and savory delicacy that's a staple of Calabrian cuisine. You would also find olives in all shapes and sizes, representing the region's rich olive growing tradition. The olive sellers take pride in offering a variety of flavors, from briny and green to ripe and black.

The bancarelle also cater to those with a sweet tooth. Many stalls are furnished with trays of cannoli, their crispy shells filled with velvety ricotta cream and dusted with powdered sugar. You'll discover an array of pastries and sweets, each more tempting than the last. Bakers showcase their skill with displays of *sfogliatelle*, flaky pastries filled with citrus-scented ricotta, and my favorite, *nocciole pralinate.* or candied hazelnuts (whole hazelnuts coated in caramelized sugar) — crunchy and sweet!

In addition to culinary delights, the bancarelle offer a treasure trove of artisanal crafts. Skilled craftsmen proudly display their creations, which often include intricate ceramics, delicate lacework, and handwoven textiles. It's an opportunity to admire the artistry and tradition that define my town and region's cultural identity.

All around the bancarelle, it's impossible not to be captivated by the festive energy that permeates the air. It becomes a place to shop and a hub of community activity, where locals and visitors come together to celebrate the region's rich heritage.

One of the most heartwarming and poignant moments I've witnessed during this feast occurred when I saw a father cradle his newborn baby high above his head, presenting the precious bundle to the statue of San Rocco. It's a tradition that has endured through generations in our town, a symbolic gesture of seeking blessings and protection for the newest members of our community.

As the father raised his child towards the statue, there was a hushed reverence in the air. The crowd, which had been abuzz with activity, fell into a respectful silence. It was as if time itself paused to witness this sacred act.

The baby, swaddled in soft blankets, gazed up at the statue with wide eyes, seemingly aware of the significance of the moment. San Rocco, decorated in his ornate robes and bearing the symbols of his patronage, looked down upon the child with a serene expression.

For that brief moment, there was a profound connection between the earthly and the divine. The father's outstretched arms and the infant's innocent trust bridged the gap between generations, reminding us of the enduring values and traditions that bind our community.

In that simple yet profound act, I saw the hopes and dreams of countless parents who wished for a bright and blessed future for their children. No matter where life may lead us, we carry the spirit of our town and the love and protection of San Rocco.

This touching scene remains as etched in my memory as the deep-rooted traditions and faith that define our town's identity. Especially nowadays, with the bustle of modern life, these experiences preserve the timeless beauty that connects us to our past and inspires us to carry forward the legacy of our ancestors.

Participating in the religious procession and the accompanying festivities every year instilled in me a sense of continuity and connection to the past. The act of carrying the statue, the sacred music, and the communal prayers taught me reverence and respect for our cultural and spiritual traditions. It brings to mind that we are part of a much larger story than our individual lives, one that spans generations and is built into our community.

I also learned how to appreciate the richness and variety of our Calabrian heritage. The symbolic tradition of presenting newborns to the statue of San Rocco showed me the importance of blessings and protection in our lives. The festival's culmination in music and dance, particularly the tarantella, as a joyful expression taught me the value of communal joy and the unifying power of shared experiences. Dancing in the streets with my neighbors, friends, and family, I understood that happiness is magnified when shared with others.

Alongside the percussive backdrop, the tarantella dancers twirl and whirl, their colorful costumes spinning as they weave intricate patterns on the cobblestone streets. The tarantella is a dance of celebration the day of the feast and fills the air with contagious exuberance.

As the statue of San Rocco makes its way toward the San Rocco church. The music adds an extra layer of emotion to the procession. It's as if the heartbeats of the town, represented by the drums and the feast spirit, embodied in the dance, converge to honor their patron saint.

The combination of visual grandeur, the scent of incense, the rhythmic drumming, and the lively tarantella creates a sensory symphony that envelops all who are fortunate enough to witness it. Music and dance become a language of reverence and celebration, uniting generations in a shared expression of faith and culture.

One evening, as the sun dipped below the horizon, casting a warm glow over our family home, my mother sat me down to share a cherished story from the past. She spoke with a fondness in her eyes and a smile that could melt any heart.

She recounted when she was expecting her first child, a time when the weight of anticipation mingled with the excitement of the unknown. She was pregnant with me, and she and my father were eager for my arrival. But as the weeks turned into days, my father couldn't contain his hopes and dreams for his unborn child, and he sought a special way to express them.

It is a tradition during the feast to play the drums as a heartfelt request to the patron saint, asking for a son when a family is expecting. It was a gesture of deep faith, a musical prayer that transcended words. So, with a heart full of hope, my father took up the drumsticks and joined the rhythmic ensemble that played in the procession.

The steady beat of the drums echoed through the streets, carrying with it the collective wishes of our family. My father, a man who loved to talk and kid around, used this moment to share his desire for a son, a cultural practice in our town, where the firstborn son often held a special place in the family's heart.

As my mother narrated this tale, I was moved by the depth of their love and the cultural significance of this tradition. The fusion of faith and heritage shaped our family's identity. The sound of those drums, played with love and devotion, had transcended time, becoming a cherished part of our family's history.

And as I sat there, listening to my mother's story, I was grateful for the path that had brought me into this world, a path marked by love, and the rhythmic heartbeat of drums that had once asked for my presence.

The sacred and the profane

I cannot overlook the intriguing and complex history that lurks beneath the surface of this beloved celebration. For generations, the 'Ndrangheta, a criminal group eradicated in Calabria that we will study in the next chapter, has wielded a subtle influence, its presence woven with the cultural and religious habits of Southern Italy.

The 'Ndrangheta, notorious for its strict code of silence and loyalty, often invoked the names of saints as a sign of commitment to its criminal brotherhood. Over the years, the criminal organization, deeply aware of the cultural and religious significance of such events, has sought to establish its presence within the traditions of Southern Italy.

They've navigated the intersections of faith, culture, and community, using these religious festivals to gain consensus within the population.

One captivating narrative recounts a peculiar phenomenon during the Festa di San Rocco's grand procession.

It is said that, in a bygone era, the statue of San Rocco would mysteriously pause and bow in profound reverence when passing the residence of the local 'Ndrangheta boss. Some interpreted this enigmatic gesture as an acknowledgment of the organization's power and influence.

To others, it was a gesture that, even in front of sanctity, made the 'Ndrangheta's presence loom large, exerting a unique authority over the town. While such accounts remain shrouded in secrecy and intrigue, they show the intricacy of faith, tradition, and the 'Ndrangheta's shadowy role within Calabria's rich cultural heritage.

These stories, while intriguing, represent only a fraction of the Festa di San Rocco's narrative. For the vast majority of participants, the celebration remains a deeply cherished and sincere expression of their faith and heritage, unburdened by the shadows that occasionally cast an unsettling aura over these age-old traditions.

During one memorable Festa di San Rocco, as the lively sounds of the tarantella dance filled the air and the streets bustled with vendors, I found myself drawn into an unexpected encounter. Amidst the colorful stalls of the bancarelle, I noticed a group of individuals discreetly approaching the owners of various market stands. These individuals, who exuded authority, were selling raffle tickets.

Curiosity awakened, I observed as they engaged in hushed conversations with the stall owners, their gestures animated and persuasive. This was no ordinary raffle; it was a discrete form of solicitation for financial contributions. While no explicit mention was made, the implicit understanding was that supporting this cause was expected, and declining was not without consequences.

As a spectator to this spectacle, I marveled at the intricacies of Calabria's social fabric. It was a delicate dance of tradition, power dynamics, and community ties unfolding before my eyes. While I remained on the periphery, I gained unique insight into the complex relationships that often underpinned the Festa di San Rocco.

In many ways, this encounter showed that the celebration, for all its vibrancy and communal spirit, was not immune to the undercurrents of influence that flowed through the region. It was a moment of intrigue among the festivities, underscoring the multifaceted nature of this cherished tradition and the intricate relationships that shaped it.

5. The 'Ndrangheta and its shapes

In this chapter, I deep-dive into the darkness of my hometown in Calabria, where organized crime, specifically the 'Ndrangheta, cast a menacing shadow over daily life. I want to convey to the reader the far-reaching influence of the 'Ndrangheta, its global presence, and its impact on both individuals and communities.

Growing up in a small town in Southern Italy was woven with both beauty and darkness. While the region was known for its breathtaking landscapes and delicious cuisine, it also bore the burden of organized crime.

Understanding the 'Ndrangheta is important for people outside of Italy too, because its activities can impact other countries. By knowing more about the group, we can better understand the challenges people in Calabria face and why it's important for governments and law enforcement agencies around the world to work together to stop its illegal activities.

The 'Ndrangheta is not a name spoken lightly in the world of organized crime. It is a powerful and secretive criminal syndicate. While the Sicilian Mafia may be more widely recognized, the 'Ndrangheta has gained notoriety for its influence and reach, both within Italy and on the global stage. Their reach spans continents, from Europe to South America, and their involvement in drug trafficking has made them a key player in the worldwide narcotics trade.

This organization started out as a local mafia many years ago but has grown to have a big impact not just in Italy, but around the world. They're involved in illegal activities like drug trafficking and money laundering, which means they make money by breaking the law in serious ways.

They operate with an iron grip, infiltrating local businesses, politics, and communities, leaving a trail of fear and corruption in their wake.

What makes the 'Ndrangheta unique and strong is the way it's organized. It's based on family ties, which means it's not just a group of people working together — it's families, often related by blood, who trust and protect each other. This makes it hard for law enforcement to fight them. The 'Ndrangheta is secretive, and because its members are often related, they're less likely to give information to the police.

In Calabria, the influence of the 'Ndrangheta can be felt in everyday life. They can have control over businesses and even influence local politics. For people living there, this can be tough because the 'Ndrangheta create a climate of fear and intimidation. But it's important to remember that not everyone in Calabria is involved with the 'Ndrangheta, and many people there don't agree with their actions and want them stopped.

The influence of this crime often impacts the younger souls. In my town, and in the whole region, a big slice of young people follow the same pattern while growing: by the age of seventeen, these youths (many of whom were my schoolmates), brimming with energy, are lured into an odyssey. It begins innocently enough with small errands, seemingly harmless tasks that slowly spiral into something darker. Under the guise of transporting "goods," these teenagers are seduced by the thrill of secret missions, the appeal of quick cash, the promise of breaking free from the confines of our town.

By nineteen, they are behind the wheel of a flashy modern Fiat 500, its white pearl exterior and red interiors symbolizing their newfound status. The trappings of this dangerous game — the sleek cars, the designer labels, the exclusive club nights — become their siren song, a heady mix of luxury and adrenaline that's impossible to resist.

At twenty-one, they're local legends — their names murmured in awe in every corner bar of the town. They walk with a swagger, in an aura of invincibility that draws admirers like moths to a flame. To the young and impressionable, icons of power and wealth, embodiments of a dream that's as intoxicating as it is perilous.

What these young people often don't realize is that the police have kept watch of them for years. The shadow of surveillance hang over their every move, their seemingly harmless journeys carrying far more weight than they could fathom. Each step they take, every covert deal they make, casts a longer, darker shadow — a shadow that's slowly closing in on them.

At twenty-four, the inevitable happens. The once untouchable heroes of our streets are led away in handcuffs, arrested, their dreams shattered by the harsh clang of prison gates — a decade, maybe more, lost to the unforgiving hands of time; years that could have been spent in the pursuit of knowledge, love, and genuine adventure.

The anger that welled up within me is, yes, for my schoolmates but also for all the young souls falling into this trap: a combination of parents who cannot properly care for them and a series of wrong decisions that alters their lives forever.

Why does this cycle keep repeating in our region? Young people, who have their whole lives ahead of them, keep making the same bad decisions. It's hard to understand. They have so many opportunities to live a good life; they could find love, get married, or go to university and learn skills for a great career but instead get caught up in a life that only leads to trouble, ending up in jail, wasting years they can never get back.

Every time I saw one of them swaggering through the streets, acting like they owned the world, a part of me felt upset. They were admired by the younger kids, who didn't know any better and thought these guys were living the dream. But I knew the truth — that the police were always watching, waiting for the right moment to catch them.

This whole situation made me think a lot about how important it is to make the right choices and to have good people around to help guide you. It also made me want to do something positive with my life and help others understand the dangers of getting involved with groups like the 'Ndrangheta.

This difficulty in our Southern Italian area isn't something new. It's a path walked by many before — fathers, grandfathers, generations of young men locked behind bars. Strangely, in our community, time spent in jail is often looked at differently. It is seen as a badge of toughness, a sign that you've been through hard times and came out stronger, rather than as a mark of failure. This way of thinking is rooted in the culture, passed down through stories shared in quiet corners and family gatherings.

Needless to say, this belief is misleading and harmful. It hides the true consequences of these choices — the dreams that are never realized, the bright futures that fade into the shadows, and the families left to deal with heartache and loss. It ignores the pain of mothers who cry for their sons, the helplessness of fathers who can't reverse time, and the strain on siblings who watch their family get torn apart. The cost of this glorified view of prison life is enormous.

This mistaken pride in enduring jail overshadows the true potential of our young people. It's a dangerous illusion that has taken too many down a path of regret. Recognizing this has made me all the more thankful for the direction I was steered in by my parents — a path that valued real achievements, education, and honesty over a misguided sense of honor.

Reflecting more on that, I'm grateful my life took a different route. My parents were always there, showing me the right way, giving me advice that made all the difference. They taught me to value education and hard work, to see that real knowledge and learning were my tickets to a better, brighter future. They showed me that true strength isn't about surviving jail. Real strength is about living a life that's honest and good, a life that helps others and makes a positive difference.

Because of their guidance, I chose a path of learning and purpose, a journey that leads to success and fulfillment. In a place where wrong choices are often glorified, I am forever thankful for the clear vision and direction my parents gave me, helping me pursue a path that truly adds value to life; a life of positive impact, in stark contrast to the shadow cast by the 'Ndrangheta over our town.

It is known that Ndrangheta's presence extends far beyond its illicit enterprises, infiltrating even the most mundane aspects of daily life.

The 'Ndrangheta's reach is a shadow that looms over local businesses. Shop owners, restaurateurs, and even market vendors often find themselves ensnared in a web of extortion. As many books narrate and YouTube videos show, the criminal organization demands a monthly fee, or "protection money."

Failure to comply with these demands carries severe consequences. The 'Ndrangheta has a repertoire of intimidation tactics, from menacing phone calls to more sinister actions. I remember that, in some instances, businesses that resisted were threatened with bombings, arson attacks, or the destruction of their livelihoods.

In my town, the presence of those involved in the shadowy world of the 'Ndrangheta was a reality we couldn't ignore. Sometimes, it was clear as day, with rumors and hushed conversations confirming

'Ndrangheta connections. Other times, the involvement was hidden behind a facade of normalcy, leaving me unaware of the true nature of my neighbors and friends.

Take Marco, for example. He was the guy next door, the sort of person you'd never suspect. He always came home before dark, while I usually stayed out late with friends. My mom used to point him out, saying, "Why can't you be more like Marco? Look how early he gets home."

But Marco had a whole other side to him. He was deep into drug dealing, a fact that stayed hidden until the police caught up with him. He ended up with a ten-year sentence. In our town, this kind of news didn't shock anyone. It was almost expected.

Years later, Marco got out of jail, and now when Mom and I talk about it, we laugh. "Remember when you wanted me to be more like Marco?" I tease. We both know how wrong we were about him.

One vivid memory from those years stands out — a night when I was working as a waiter in a renowned pizzeria in town. The pizzeria was bustling with patrons, the air thick with the aroma of freshly made pizzas. Families gathered around tables, laughter and chatter filling the space.

Amid the lively atmosphere, a man entered the pizzeria, his appearance somewhat unsettling. He ordered a selection of pizzas for his family, and the total came to forty-six euros.

When it came time to settle the bill, he approached the cashier, who was also the owner of the pizzeria, with a sly smile.

The man handed thirty-five euros to the owner, his eyes locked on the cashier's with unwavering determination. The room held its breath as the two engaged in a silent standoff. Then, with a smirk, the man turned and left the pizzeria, his parting words dripping with sarcasm. "This is enough," he said with an air of superiority, as if he could dictate the terms and pay as he saw fit. This gesture carried the nonchalant confidence of those affiliated with the 'Ndrangheta.

The owner of the pizzeria, a veteran of such encounters, knew better than to challenge the man openly. Instead, he accepted the thirty-five euros with a forced smile, his eyes betraying a mixture of resignation and anger.

In a surprisingly generous gesture considering the circumstances, the man left me a one-euro tip.

I chuckle at the irony of the situation. Here was a man willing to shortchange a restaurant by not paying the full amount, yet he still left a tip — albeit a modest one. The influence of the 'Ndrangheta often permeated everyday interactions in peculiar and unpredictable ways.

Fast forward a few years to a sunny day at the Ionian beach with my brothers. We were enjoying the clear waters, kids playing in the sand, and the relaxed atmosphere of my favorite beach club. But despite the serenity, I noticed a group of men on a boat approaching dangerously close to the shore, where children were playing.

Concerned for the safety of the kids, I raise my voice, yelling at the men to keep their boat away from the shore. One of them, a stern looking individual, went back from the passenger seat of the boat to the helm, anchored the boat at a distance, and then swam to shore.

After a while, he walked through the beach, and came closer to my umbrella, where my brothers and I were happily drinking a cocktail. He demanded to know who I was; for us Calabrians, not an odd question in the circumstances.

To my surprise, the man asked me to accompany him, insisting he needed to speak with me privately. I hesitated at first, telling him that if he had something to say, he should say it now. Undeterred, he got closer and revealed that he was a well-known figure in our town.

He continued talking but realized he was a close friend of my cousin and had a good relationship with my brothers. Understanding the connections, I felt a mixture of relief and curiosity. The tension diffused as we spoke further, and we eventually shared a drink together, the animosity of our initial encounter giving way to a funny story.

This encounter at the beach illustrates a prevalent trait in our town — ignorance. Many hadn't had the opportunity for education, and ignorance often led to quick tempers and conflicts. In such a community, it was easy for tensions to escalate, especially when dealing with outsiders.

6. The variety of families in town

The town I call home is structured with families of diverse backgrounds and roles. Each family brings its unique thread to this puzzle, shaping the culture and identity of the town. As I walk its streets and witness daily life, I notice the subtle distinctions that set each family apart.

In this chapter, I'll introduce you to these various South Italian families, from the families of doctors and lawyers to the families deeply connected to the land, the artisans, and even the enigmatic families associated with the 'Ndrangheta. Together, they form the rich, complex essence of our town.

The families of doctors and lawyers

The families of doctors and lawyers, who graced our town with prestige and intellectual vigor, instilled in their children a profound respect for education, equipping them with dreams of becoming legal or medical professionals. These children were often the top students in our school, distinguished by their ambition and sophistication.

One of my closest friends from this category was Alex, a classmate who shared my love for adventure and gaming. Her father, a renowned lawyer in our town, was well respected for his legal acumen.

Alex and I used to spend afternoons after school playing Nintendo at her house, engrossed in epic battles and shared laughter. As we explored the virtual worlds of video games, Alex would share stories about her family's legal legacy. She used to talk about her father's courtroom wins and how she aspired to follow in his footsteps. Despite the seriousness of her family's profession, Alex had an infectious sense of humor. She'd joke that her dad argued cases with the same passion she demonstrated in our video game battles.

Our friendship transcended social and economic boundaries, highlighting the rich mixture of our town. Through Alex, I learned that success came in many forms, and dreams were not limited by one's background. The families of doctors and lawyers showed that excellence was attainable through hard work and knowledge, forging connections that could break down barriers and broaden horizons.

Alex's journey through life led her to become a respected lawyer like her father. She demonstrated that even within the most accomplished families, there was room for dreams. These families instilled in their children a commitment to intellectual excellence as well as a sense of community that transcended their professional achievements.

The families of the land

Then there were the families of the land, those who owned the knowledge of the agricultural traditions of Calabria. They were the quiet powerhouses, tending to acres of fertile soil, cultivating orchards, and nurturing vineyards. The fruits of their hard work graced the tables of our town, nourishing the body and soul.

One such family, the Giancettis, had been cultivating the land for generations. It was a warm summer's day, and I recall visiting their sprawling farm as a young boy. The Giancettis children, my friends, always brimmed with enthusiasm and energy. As we ran through the fields, they taught me about the delicate balance of nature, about sowing, reaping, and the strong bond between a farmer and his land.

What set these families apart was their dedication to education. While their days began with the rising sun and were filled with the tireless toiling of the fields, they devoted their evenings to books and learning. I remember the Giancetti children's father, Vincenzo, insisting on the importance of education, his hands gently turning the pages of textbooks.

Many other families of the land echoed this. They believed a strong education was a path to brighter opportunities, even if those opportunities led beyond the fields. As the Giancetti children grew, they each pursued higher education and professions away from the land, while Vincenzo remained a proud steward of the farm.

This emphasis on education provided its fruit. The children of these families became doctors, lawyers, and engineers, bringing their knowledge and experiences back to our town. They were the pillars of progress, combining their respect for traditions with a commitment to modernity.

In the middle of a town defined by its contrasts, the families of the land were the bridge between tradition and innovation, their influence spreading far beyond the fields they tilled. They exemplified how, with dedication and discipline, one could cultivate crops in parallel with the future of our community.

These families taught me that the intrinsic connection between the land and its people was nurturing the potential within each child, sowing the seeds of a bright future.

The families of artisans

My own family belonged to this category, with my father working as a barber and my mother as a hairdresser. Artisan families were the backbone of the local economy, an example of passion and dedication, contributing to the town's unique character through their trades.

Artisan parents understood the importance of passing down their skills and knowledge to their children, often starting the education in their workshops at a young age. My parents were no different. From the age of six, I used to sweep the floors of my father's barbershop and watch with fascination as he worked his magic with scissors and razors. I absorbed valuable lessons in craftsmanship, dedication, and the importance of building personal connections with clients.

In these families, education wasn't limited to formal schools. My parents, like many others in our town, believed that a strong work ethic and a genuine love for one's situation could serve as a foundation for a prosperous life. I learned how by cultivating passions that greatly contributed to cultivating a sane life.

While I witnessed my parents shaping the lives of our neighbors, I also observed other artisan families excelling in their respective trades. Local potters, tailors, and bakers displayed a similar commitment to their businesses, taking pride in their work and believing true success lay in the art of creation.

The children of artisans carried forward the dedication, recognizing the importance of upholding age-old techniques while adapting to modern demands, becoming the inheritors of skills that had been refined over generations.

In our town, it wasn't uncommon to see children from artisan families rise to great heights, taking over their parents' businesses or establishing new ventures. Of course, financial success came with discipline.

Through the efforts of these families of artisans, our town maintained its distinct cultural identity, as they enriched our lives through their art and the educational values they granted their children. My parents, like others in our town, emphasized that dedication, passion, and a love for what one does were the keys to a prosperous and fulfilling life.

These families made me realize that it's okay to follow your own path, even if it's different from what others expect, and they showed me that finding joy in what you do, every day, is one of the most important things in life. That's something I've carried with me, always.

Guess what… Well, in the shadowy world of the 'Ndrangheta as well, families can be classified into two distinct groups. I'd like to make up these labels to identify the two categories with the promise to transmit an accurate essence of both: the Silent Guardians and the Flamboyant Figures.

The Silent Guardians

In the subtle undertones of 'Ndrangheta, an archetype exists; one that operates like a shadow, unnoticed by most. I call them the Silent Guardians, the families who prefer to keep low profiles, understanding that power often thrives in obscurity.

Their houses are modest, blending seamlessly into the neighborhood. Their cars, while well maintained, don't scream luxury. These families avoid the extravagant gatherings, parties, and flamboyance that the Flamboyant Figures embrace.

A perfect example of Flamboyant Figures is the family who lived just down the street from our home. Believe me, they were friendly neighbors, always ready to offer a helping hand, especially when it came to community events. Despite their unassuming exterior, they held a significant presence within the 'Ndrangheta. *L'abito non fa il monaco*, is translated literally as "the dress does not make the priest," or more commonly, "christened wine doesn't go with the palate."

One summer evening, I happened to witness, hidden behind a thicket of bushes, an unexpected reunion. With the sun setting, the garden seemed like a secret meeting place.

The group of people exchanged hushed words, and as I strained to monitor them, I recognized this was not an ordinary meeting.

I already knew this family was known for their discretion. They were the Silent Guardians, ensuring that the town and neighboring towns operated together under the influence of the 'Ndrangheta. They had the responsibility to maintain a certain balance of power, ensuring that the organization's interests were protected without drawing unnecessary attention from people or police forces.

As a kid, of course, I was both scared and fascinated. Can you picture it? It was like discovering a hidden world right in our own neighborhood. The real lesson out of this experience was to be more aware and observant, to look beyond the surface. I learned that the real power often lies in being unnoticed, in keeping things low key.

Living in this kind of environment, where nothing is quite as simple as it looks, shaped the way I view the world. It made me cautious and thoughtful about who I trust and how I see people. It also influenced my character, teaching me the importance of being discreet and understanding the deeper layers of any situation.

This background has made me realize that true strength and influence don't always need to be loud or showy. Sometimes, they're most effective when they're quiet and hidden, just like the Silent Guardians in our town.

I always thought the Silent Guardians were an integral component of the 'Ndrangheta's operations, for while the Flamboyant Figures made headlines and the Artisans carried out the organization's covert activities, it was the Silent Guardians who kept the wheels turning.

They probably understood that their influence was more potent when obscured by the facade of normalcy, making them an enigmatic force in the town's complex dough.

The Flamboyant Figures

Within the secretive domain of the 'Ndrangheta, the Flamboyant Figures were an intriguing breed. They were who decided that, "If you're going to be involved, you might as well show your status." These families often lived in huge mansions tucked away on the outskirts of town, and their choice of vehicles was extravagant. Luxury cars, gleaming with richness, rolled down our narrow cobblestone streets, drawing people's attention.

There was one family in particular known for hosting the most luxurious parties and gatherings. When they threw a celebration at their mansion, the entire region anticipated the event. Their grand villa showed their wealth, with spreading gardens that were filled with an array of guests; some local, others from distant corners of the country.

As a kid, I once snuck a peek inside a grand mansion during a local festival. This house was something else. With its towering pillars and fancy chandeliers, it was like stepping into another world. I wondered why everything was so extravagant. The clear swimming pool and the beautiful paintings on the walls were dazzling.

These parties weren't just regular gatherings; they were a chance for the family to show off their wealth and status. Listening in on their conversations, I heard them talk about expensive cars and trips to exotic places. I thought, did they really need to show off so much? They seemed to love letting everyone know how wealthy they were. But their lifestyle was a balancing act. They were both admired and feared. How did they handle this double-edged sword of admiration and fear?

Their flashy way of living was like an unspoken announcement of their place within the 'Ndrangheta. Why did people avoid crossing their path, and what did this say about our town? They served as a constant reminder that Calabria, while beautiful, also had a complicated and secret-filled side.

In our town, every family played a unique role, like different threads in a tapestry. But what was the true influence of the 'Ndrangheta families always lurking in the background? How did other families contribute to the complex picture that defined our community?

The way different families got along was pretty interesting. The 'Ndrangheta families, who were kind of secretive and powerful, always had a quiet way of influencing things around town. You couldn't always see it, but it was there.

Then there were families like mine, the artisans. We were known for our activities and were a big part of everyday life in town. We were all about keeping old traditions going and making sure our community stayed amicable. Our lives were different from the 'Ndrangheta families, who were more about staying hidden and having control.

Even though we were different, all of us in the town depended on each other in some way. The rich families would often use the services that our artisan families offered. This kind of need for each other made sure we all had a place in the town.

Living side by side, even if it was a bit tricky at times, helped our town work. It was like a big puzzle where each family, whether quiet and powerful or open and traditional, had their own important piece. This mix of different families and lifestyles made our town a special place with its own unique feel.

7. A Journey to knowledge

In this chapter, I take you through my journey from the humble beginnings in Calabria to the challenging halls of higher education. I'd like to share how my simple upbringing has shaped my path and how the lessons learned in my early days in Calabria have become the cornerstone of my pursuit for academic and personal growth. As I navigate through the trials of school and university, I'm constantly reflecting: How does my Calabrian heritage influence my ambitions and resilience? I will explore how my roots in Calabria have given me the strength and determination to thrive in a world much bigger than the one I grew up in.

High school marked a significant chapter in my life. I embarked on this educational journey at a technical high school. The school was located a mere fifteen minutes away; a daily expedition that brought challenges and memorable moments.

My day would typically commence early in the morning. To ensure a smooth pick up by my uncle, Zio Totó, who worked at the school, I'd make my way to the bus stop from home. In front of the bus stop, friends and fellow schoolmates would gather, all with the same intention — to catch a ride to school. The bus ticket cost around three euros, and it was essential to factor in a bus change during the journey. This made the prospect of catching rides particularly appealing.

For several months, my uncle's presence as my ride was a boon. His car would pull up, and I would hop in, letting the others hoping for a lift join. The convenience of avoiding the bus fare and the hassle of transfers was a welcome respite during this period.

One morning, I overslept, and time slipped away faster than I could manage. As I rushed to the bus stop, I could already see my uncle's car waiting impatiently with the engine running. I sprinted to catch up, my backpack bouncing behind me, and just as I reached the car, I saw the exasperated expression on my uncle's face.

"Sorry, sorry, I lost track of time," I said as I slid into the passenger seat.

My uncle let out an exaggerated sigh. "You're going to make me late for work."

In my haste, I had, indeed, disrupted his tuned routine. We let in the line of students waiting for a ride, but this time, I could feel my classmates' smirks. They were all too aware of my comedic delay.

The way back was a bit different. My uncle used to leave earlier than when us regular students got out of class, due to the nature of his job. This meant I was forced to take the bus back to my town.

One day, as the school bus drove its return route, I sat next to my schoolmate, Rocco. He possessed a laid back attitude toward education. He attended school, not out of a burning desire for knowledge, but simply to appease his parents. Education, for him, was more an obligation than a passion.

One of those days, during our bus ride, an impressive BMW Z4 caught my eye. I swear, it was sleek, powerful, and radiated sophistication. My youthful enthusiasm got the best of me, and I turned to Rocco with a glint of determination in my eyes, declaring, "I will buy a car like that soon."

Rocco, with his characteristic nonchalance and a hint of amusement, turned to me. "You?" he asked, a smirk playing on his lips. "You'll never be able to buy one of those. You should probably go home and take a nap instead."

Rocco's words, though lighthearted, made a profound impact on me. It was like a bolt of lightning; a moment that felt almost traumatic. Strangely, it was this very moment that sparked an unquenchable fire within me.

The BMW Z4 became the symbol of dreams, aspirations, and the resilience to chase them. This seemingly trivial exchange on a bus ride would go on to transform my future endeavors, marking in me an unhesitating determination.

To this day, that memory is still vivid; proof of the power of dreams and the impact of a few words exchanged in passing. Even the loftiest ambitions can be achieved with dedication and the refusal to give up.

My journey through life led me to a pivotal crossroads after completing high school. My parents pushed me toward deciding to continue my education, recognizing the incredible opportunity that lay before me. In Italy, higher education is accessible to those with lower family incomes, making it an open door for those willing to pursue it. So, why not take a chance?

The path I chose led me to the city of Cosenza and the University of Calabria. This university became my new home for almost five years, and the ease of learning became my constant companion. The transition from a small town to a vibrant academic environment was exciting and daunting at the same time.

My chosen field of study was electronics engineering, a discipline that promised to unlock the mysteries of the modern world. The campus was huge, and it buzzed with students from diverse backgrounds, all driven by shared passions.

The journey to the university was a daily adventure. The university was a three-hour drive from my home, which meant I could only return on weekends, and sometimes even less frequently. This experience was marked by a relentless pursuit of knowledge. I immersed myself in the world of electronics engineering, absorbing the intricacies.

The professors were passionate about their subjects, and their enthusiasm was infectious. In due course, I earned my bachelor's degree, a significant milestone in my academic journey. Additionally, I hungered for more and decided to embark on the path of a master's degree. This next logical step demanded even more dedication and determination.

From the early days of my bachelor's degree, I was acutely aware of the significance of striking a balance between academic excellence and the development of essential interpersonal skills. These skills, I understood, were invaluable assets as I embarked on a journey that would eventually lead me into the professional realm.

With this learning, I set out to excel in my studies and to feed my ability to connect with others, building relationships that would prove indispensable in the business world.

During this period of academic growth and social exploration, I organized gatherings and memorable parties with my friends. These events, filled with food, drinks, and shared experiences, became an integral part of our university life.

I remained committed to my studies and academic goals; however, I firmly believed that a well-rounded education extended beyond textbooks and lecture halls. It encompassed the cultivation of interpersonal skills, an aspect of learning that I recognized as equally vital for success in any career.

As I delved into my university courses, a passion emerged as a sanctuary of joy and social interaction. Salsa dancing.

It was a refreshing escape from textbooks and lectures, where I could express myself freely and connect with others on a different plane. The rhythm and energy of salsa enriched my university experience and nurtured a growing love for this art form.

Recognizing an opportunity, I began teaching salsa, turning my passion into a practical way to support myself through university. Teaching salsa allowed me to refine my interpersonal skills, both as a dancer and as an instructor, while providing a joyful diversion from the rigors of academic life.

The years that followed provided ample evidence of the wisdom in this approach.

In fact, many of my peers, who had dedicated themselves solely to academic pursuits, found employment but often encountered challenges in reaching their full potential. This made me reflect. It became clear that the ability to connect with others, forge meaningful relationships, and navigate the intricacies of social dynamics was as crucial as academic mastery.

So important were the friendships and connections I made, they enriched my emotional intelligence. I learned the impact of empathy and teamwork, and the art of building lasting relationships. These skills, developed outside the classroom, were crucial in improving my ability to interact and connect with others.

Many people contributed to shaping my life during school. Often, I reflect on the significant role my dear friend, Edo, played in my formative years. Edo was a childhood friend and like a brother. We shared countless memories, dreams, and aspirations as we navigated the path of life together.

During the summers, when academic demands temporarily eased, Edo and I would put on our bartender shirts and work together. We mixed cocktails, listened to the laughter of tourists, and found our own brand of happiness in the chaos of the bar. Edo's presence was a constant source of inspiration. He had a fervor for investments and innovation, always searching for the next big opportunity. He was a dreamer, and his dreams were infectious.

One unforgettable memory that encapsulates Edo's and my shared journey as friends, dreamers, and co-workers revolves around our unexpected venture as DJs. It was a wild idea born out of our shared passion for music and the desire to create something extraordinary. We decided to organize a party; a bold move we thought would be a small-scale affair, mainly attended by friends and a handful of locals.

As the day of the event approached, we wondered if we had bitten off more than we could chew. Uncertainty grew within us. We were not seasoned DJs, and the expectations for the party were high. We had invested our energy, creativity, and a bit of savings into this task. Yet, the question lingered: Would anyone even show up?

The evening arrived, and we set up the equipment, fine tuning the playlist and creating an atmosphere we hoped would be inviting. Initially, the venue seemed almost deserted. Our hearts dropped, and self-doubt whispered that we might have made a colossal mistake. But

Edo, true to his nature, remained undeterred, reminding me that every dream begins with a leap of faith.

Then, it happened. Out of nowhere, the tide began to turn. People started to come in. The atmosphere changed as the music flowed from our fingertips. The initial spill transformed into a flood, and the party took on a life of its own. The crowd was far larger than we had anticipated. We watched in amazement as strangers danced and celebrated life, all united by the music and energy we had created.

Edo and I spun records, working in harmony, and the once quiet venue had transformed into a pulsating party of music. That night, we realized that sometimes, all it takes is a little courage, faith, and passion to turn a simple idea into something extraordinary.

The success of that night became symbolic of our shared dreams, of what we could achieve when we believed in ourselves and each other. It was an unforgettable night that encapsulated our friendship, our dreams, and the incredible journey we had embarked on together.

As time went on, our paths diverged. I embarked on a journey to the United States, seeking academic progress and professional success. My pursuit of career opportunities took me far from our Calabrian roots. Edo, on the other hand, chose a different route; one that led him to a loving wife and two beautiful children.

Despite the physical distance that now separated us, our friendship remained strong. Edo's support and belief in me during those early days of striving for success were invaluable. I admire his choices and the life he has built.

The years I spent at university, juggling intense academic work and social interactions, deeply impacted me emotionally and in the development of my character. The long commutes and rare visits home made me appreciate the value of time and the importance of balancing different aspects of my life.

The late nights of studying and experimenting, driven by my passion to excel, taught me discipline and perseverance. These qualities became part of who I am, shaping me into someone who faces challenges head-on.

Moreover, these experiences, academic and social, played a crucial role in shaping my character, preparing me for the complexities of the professional world and life's unpredictable journey, gifting me a deeper understanding of myself and the world around me.

As I progressed in my academic journey, an exceptional opportunity presented itself: the Erasmus program. This remarkable initiative aimed to facilitate cultural exchange and mutual understanding among

European university students. It was a chance to broaden my horizons in the most humbling way.

Erasmus, named after the renowned Dutch philosopher Erasmus of Rotterdam, is a program that holds immense promise. It allows European students to study abroad, immersing themselves in different cultures and forging connections with peers from across the globe.

As a diligent student, I was fortunate to be eligible for this transformative experience, with the university generously covering my tuition and expenses.

My destination was Slovakia, a land steeped in history and culture, where I would spend over a year of my academic journey. The prospect of exploring a new part of Europe was irresistible, and I embarked on this adventure with boundless enthusiasm.

One of the most remarkable facets of the Erasmus experience was the opportunity it provided to connect with students from all corners of the world. Slovakia, with its diverse student community, brought together individuals with unique stories and backgrounds, fostering friendships that transcended borders.

During my time in Slovakia, a particularly memorable evening unfolded despite the backdrop of freezing temperatures. This was a cold that I had never experienced (until later on in Michigan, North America). The bitter cold served as the backdrop to an unforgettable encounter. Some newfound friends from different parts of the world and I decided to brave the weather and embark on a peculiar drinking adventure.

In Slovakia, with my new friend, Claudio, we discovered a local concoction known as Mongolia. It was a drink with embedded layers of overlapping flavors — beer, Coca Cola, and vodka. To fully embrace the experience, we had to drink it all at once. As we clinked glasses and took those daring sips, we laughed at the unexpected medley of flavors.

That frigid night, as we huddled together to stay warm and savored the peculiar combination of Mongolia, it became apparent that the Erasmus experience had helped me forge connections; embracing the unfamiliar and creating memories that would stay with us long after we returned to our respective homelands.

The Erasmus program had opened doors to friendships that spanned the globe, enriching my life with diverse perspectives and unforgettable moments. It was a chapter in my academic journey that went beyond textbooks and lectures, teaching me the true value of global connections and the beauty of shared experiences.

Here, I also had the privilege of sharing a dormitory with students from around the globe. Our dormitory had a shared kitchen, a melting pot of culinary traditions and tastes. It was in this very kitchen that I witnessed a clash of cultures that left a lasting impression.

One evening, a friend from Afghanistan, devoted to his religion, entered the kitchen to find a French student in the middle of cooking a dish that posed a significant dilemma — pork, forbidden by Islamic dietary laws. Without hesitation, my Afghan friend took action. He grabbed the pan containing the offending meal and sent the entire contents flying out the kitchen window from our fifth-floor vantage point.

It was an incident that left us all in shock, but it also opened our minds to a profound discussion on cultural sensitivities and the importance of understanding and respecting one another's beliefs. In that shared kitchen, we learned to appreciate diverse perspectives and to navigate the complexities of living in a multicultural environment.

This story somehow marked my life, and taught me that when we step out of our comfort zones and into the wider world, we encounter opportunities for personal growth as well as the chance to bridge cultural gaps and build connections that transcend borders.

It's through such experiences that we truly unlock a world of learning and understanding, going beyond the confines of academia, absorbing the profound lesson about the boundless opportunities that life has to offer, and laying the foundation for a brilliant future.

I learnt how, in a world that is increasingly interconnected, the ability to navigate different cultures and communicate with people from various walks of life is an invaluable skill. The friendships forged during my time in Slovakia were those fleeting connections, fundamental to a global network that would serve me well in the years to come.

8. From Italy to the US: my journey abroad

In this chapter, I share my experiences transitioning from Italy to the United States. How does a young man from Calabria adapt to life in America? I recount my initial challenges with language and cultural differences, exploring how these experiences shaped my understanding and adaptation to a new way of life.

How did I navigate the new social norms, from understanding the local dialect to embracing hobbies like fishing and understanding American customer service? Each of these experiences brought new insights, helping me integrate into American society. This chapter is a reflection of my journey from the familiar streets of Calabria to the new and exciting challenges in America, marking another significant leap towards my dream of making it in Silicon Valley.

After finishing university, I started my first job in Italy as a test engineer in a semiconductor company. What excitement! I worked there for nearly two years, learning a lot and enjoying my work. But deep down, I knew I wanted more. I had a big dream to travel and work abroad. So, I started looking for jobs outside Italy, never giving up, even when it was tough.

My hard work paid off when I got a job offer from the United States, in a small but amazing town called Ann Arbor, Michigan, working for a huge company as an electrical engineer. Moving there — my first time in the US — was a huge change. It was exciting but also a bit scary, as, here in Ann Arbor, I started learning new things every day about American life and culture.

One of the biggest challenges was getting used to speaking English — not the kind I learned in Europe, but the real, everyday English people speak in the US. It was funny sometimes, and other times a bit confusing, trying to understand all the new words and the way people talked.

To connect better with people and feel more comfortable in social situations, I had to improve my communication. I worked hard on my English, not just speaking it, but also understanding the local expressions and humor.

During my initial time in the US, I often chose to listen more than talk and was held back by the fear of making grammar mistakes or mispronouncing words in English. It was a silent battle with my confidence, as I absorbed the complexities of a new language in everyday conversations.

I discovered the power of patience and the value of surrounding myself with supportive people. My group of coworkers, who quickly became like family to me in the US, played a crucial role in this journey. With their encouragement and understanding, I gradually found my voice. They created a space where I felt safe to try, make mistakes, and learn. Over time, my fears faded, replaced by a growing confidence in my ability to communicate.

As I became more comfortable with the English language, I spoke more and began to imitate the pronunciation and the North American accent, which I absolutely fell in love with. There was something about the way the words flowed and the distinct sounds of the "Great Lakes" accent that captivated me.

I would listen to my colleagues, observing the nuances of their speech, and then try to replicate them in my own conversations. The more I practiced, the more natural it felt, and soon, I started noticing that my accent was changing, slowly taking on the tones and rhythms of those around me.

As I adapted to the North American accent and lifestyle, I also discovered common hobbies here in North America, like hunting and fishing — activities quite different from what I was used to in Italy. Of course, the goal was to learn how people around me did things. I paid attention to how my colleagues at work talked to each other, how they held meetings, and even how they took breaks. I needed to understand the American way of doing things.

I began exploring new sports, starting with fishing, alongside my group of friends.

These fishing trips turned out to be quite an interesting experience for me. We would spend hours by the water, chatting and waiting for a catch.

But what I found amusing was what happened next — we often threw the caught fish back into the water. This was quite different from back home in Italy, where a caught fish usually meant a fresh meal. This practice led me to ponder: Is fishing in the United States more about the sport than the catch? Are there other hobbies and customs here that might seem just as unusual to a newcomer?

This approach to integration — spending time with locals and participating in their hobbies — was proving to be the best way for me to feel part of this new world. Each of these experiences, like the catch-and-release fishing, brought new questions and insights about American culture.

How do Americans perceive their relationship with nature through these activities? And how do these hobbies reflect the broader values and lifestyle of the community here? These questions made each new activity an opportunity for deeper understanding and appreciation of my new home.

My exploration of North American hobbies naturally led to an observation of another distinct aspect of life here — housing and the way people live. Coming from Italy, where towns are often characterized by houses huddled close together, historical centers, and limited open space, the contrast in Michigan was striking.

I transitioned from the compact, community-centric living of Italy to the expansive, almost spacious lifestyle in Michigan, where distances between places were larger and vast fields were a common sight.

In North America, I noticed how the concept of a home extended beyond just the structure itself. There, having a home with a backyard and a grill seemed almost essential; a huge difference from the living quarters back in Italy. This observation led me to think about the cultural significance of such living spaces. What does this emphasis on space and privacy say about American culture? How does the luxury of space influence family life and social gatherings here?

In Italy, the limited space often translated to a more communal way of life, where interactions with neighbors and the community were an everyday affair. In contrast, the spacious homes of Michigan, with their large backyards, seemed to offer a different kind of lifestyle, one that perhaps prioritized personal space and individual comfort.

This difference in living arrangements made me curious about the various ways people create their living environments and how these spaces reflect the values and lifestyles of their cultures. It was fascinating to see how something as fundamental as housing could offer such insights into the contrasting Italian and American ways of life.

After getting used to life in the United States and learning about its culture, I decided to take another big step. A few years after moving, I had the opportunity to go back to school and get another master's degree. This time, I chose to study business program management.

This was a key to unlocking a deeper understanding of the world of business, especially with a plan to head to the tech heartland, Silicon Valley.

I was about to dig into the art of strategy, team leadership, and project organization; skills I had seen my managers handle with impressive finesse. Their ability to go through complex business situations with such skill had left an impression on me. How did they make it look so effortless? Could I learn to do the same?

School life, however, wasn't all serious business. It came with its share of comical hiccups and learning moments. Picture this: I'm in the middle of a crucial presentation, and suddenly, my phone decides it's the perfect time to serenade the room with salsa music. Or that early morning mix-up — who schedules a team meeting for 2:00 am? Well, apparently, I do. It's these moments, though, that stick with you, teaching you lessons no textbook ever could.

Every lecture, every assignment, was a step closer to understanding what it took to be a great leader in business. Could I mirror the organizational abilities of my managers? Could I steer a project to success like they did? It was like putting together pieces of a puzzle, with each new skill and bit of knowledge, I was building my ability to make an impact in the tech industry.

I often wondered if I could really apply these lessons in the real world. How would I handle the pressures and challenges of managing complex projects? The journey through this degree was both academic growth and a test of my potential to evolve into the kind of leader I admired. With every new challenge, I inched closer to those answers, armed with newfound knowledge and a dash of salsa spirit.

After several years in the United States, I began to reflect on the nuances of building friendships here compared to Italy, pondering why it seemed more challenging. My observations aligned with some cultural insights and findings in social literature.

In Italy, the cultural structure is based on extended social interactions that often take place in public settings like cafes, bars, or town squares late into the night. These environments naturally foster social connections and prolonged conversations, crucial elements for deepening friendships.

In contrast, American social culture, as noted in various sociological studies, tends to value efficiency and individualism, which is reflected in how social interactions are built. For instance, the early closing hours of bars and restaurants in the US mirrors a lifestyle that is often more scheduled and segmented.

This difference can limit the spontaneous, lengthy gatherings that characterize Italian social life. Additionally, I noticed that American society places a strong emphasis on privacy and personal space, which, while respecting individual boundaries, can sometimes create barriers to the fluid, open-ended social interactions more common in Italian culture.

With my new skills and growing confidence in business, I started to think more about making friends in the US and how different it was from back home. This was something I really noticed as I settled into my new life.

I reflect on this: the US is a vast and diverse country where people often move for work or education, like I did, leading to more transient communities. This mobility can impact the formation of long-term relationships. In contrast, many Italian communities are more stable and multigenerational, with deep-rooted social networks that are conducive to forming strong, enduring friendships.

Understanding these cultural differences has provided me with insights into the friendship formation in different societies. It has also emphasized the importance of adapting one's social approach to the cultural context, recognizing that each culture has unique ways of fostering relationships.

Staying flexible was key, too. Sometimes things were done differently than back home, so I had to be adaptable and not get stuck on "the way I'm used to." This flexibility helped me a lot at work, especially when in teams or adjusting to new projects.

Overall, my strategy was to be observant, work on my communication, share my own culture, and stay flexible. These approaches really helped me quickly adapt to life and work in America.

With my growing understanding of life in the US, I appreciated certain aspects of American culture, particularly the way customers were treated. There's a saying that "the customer is always right," and I experienced this in a way that was surprising and quite different from what I was used to in Italy.

One day, I was at a grocery store picking up some juice. When I reached the checkout counter, I noticed that the price seemed higher than what was stated on the shelf. Back in Italy, a discrepancy like this would typically involve a lengthy discussion or a trip back to the shelf to verify the price. But here, it played out differently. I mentioned the difference to the lady at the counter, half expecting her to ask for proof or to go check the shelf herself. Instead, she simply smiled and said, "I can do that for you" and promptly changed the price to what I had seen. She trusted my word without any questions, something almost unheard of back home.

After, I called my mom to tell her what happened. I laughed as I explained how the cashier just changed the price because I said it was different. My mom was just as surprised. We both laughed about it. It was so funny to think about how easy and trusting everything was here in the US.

This simple experience at the grocery store had a surprising impact on me, leaving me with a mix of amusement and a deep sense of wonder. It was such a small moment, yet it spoke volumes about the trust and ease of everyday interactions in America, a huge contrast to what I was used to back in Italy.

This incident made me feel welcomed and trusted as well, as it opened my eyes to the cultural differences in handling everyday situations. It felt heartwarming and perplexing to realize how a small act of trust could be so impactful.

Sharing this story with my mom and hearing her surprise too brought a sense of closeness despite the distance, as we both marveled at this new, simpler way of life.

I reflected on the cultural difference between the United States and Europe, particularly in customer service. This difference is rooted in various business practices and consumer expectations, as narrated in numerous studies and business literature.

The American market, characterized by a strong emphasis on customer satisfaction, often prioritizes the customer's perception and experience, shows that the concept of customer service is deeply connected to the business spirit, and is often seen as a key differentiator in the market. This approach is sustained by the philosophy that exceptional customer service leads to customer loyalty, which is crucial in this competitive market.

In contrast, European customer service tends to be more transactional and less focused on the individual customer's experience. This isn't to say that customer service isn't important in Europe, but that the approach is different. European businesses often emphasize the quality of their products or the expertise of their service, with less focus on tailoring the experience to individual customer needs or resolving issues based on customer feedback alone.

I learned that American businesses invest heavily in customer service training and empower employees to make decisions that improve customer satisfaction, as seen in my experience at the grocery store. This level of empowerment is less common in European business settings, where procedures and protocols often take precedence over individual discretion.

Well, now that I'd been integrated into society after a substantial amount of time in America, it was time for another big move. Sadly leaving my North American friends in Michigan, I headed southwest.

My unwavering dream, Silicon Valley, was my goal — the heart of the tech world.

I accepted a job offer into one of the most promising and advanced tech companies focused on autonomous driving. Believe me, I was amazed by how tech companies treated their employees there. It was like nothing I'd ever seen. These companies made sure their employees were comfortable and happy at work. I had never experienced anything like this back in Italy or even in other parts of the US. It was a whole new world for me, seeing how these big tech companies really cared about making their employees feel great.

In Europe, companies often prioritize tradition, stability, and professionalism. The workplace is formal, with a clear line between personal and professional life. This approach has its strengths, promoting a sense of reliability and respect for established methods. But in Silicon Valley, the workplace culture is almost revolutionary by comparison. Here, companies blur the lines between work and personal life. They create environments where employees feel relaxed and inspired, with free meals, casual workspaces, and an overall emphasis on comfort and creativity.

This approach raises intriguing questions. Does this more-relaxed atmosphere actually lead to greater innovation and productivity? How does the blending of personal and professional life affect the overall wellbeing of employees?

These tech companies in Silicon Valley seem to operate on the belief that a happy employee is a more effective and creative one. This mindset is a shift from the European emphasis on maintaining professionalism and traditional structures. It makes me wonder, could

European companies benefit from adopting some of these practices? How would such a shift impact the long-standing business cultures in Europe?

In Silicon Valley, there's a relentless pursuit of innovation, constantly pushing boundaries, and this is mirrored in how they approach employee welfare. In contrast, Europe's respect for tradition and established practices provides a different kind of stability and predictability.

Both cultures offer valuable insights, but experiencing the Silicon Valley way was refreshing and eye-opening for me. It still begs the question, what can these two different worlds learn from each other to create more dynamic, supportive, and innovative workplaces?

This contrast between the two worlds broadened my understanding of global business practices and sparked a curiosity about how blending these approaches could lead to more holistic and effective work environments.

This difference made me reflect deeply on my own working style and values. In Silicon Valley, I adapted to this new environment, learning to embrace comfort and creativity in my work. I challenged myself to rethink my assumptions about work-life balance and the nature of innovation.

The Silicon Valley culture encouraged me to be more open-minded and flexible, traits that have since become integral to my professional identity, prompting me to consider the importance of employee well-being and happiness, which I hadn't fully appreciated before.

I expanded my professional skills and enriched my personal life, learning the value of a supportive work environment. I saw how blending the best of both worlds — the innovative spirit of Silicon Valley and the traditional structure of European business — could lead to a more fulfilling and effective career path.

As I navigated this cultural shift, it became clear that such experiences were crucial in shaping a more adaptable, innovative, and well-rounded professional.

9. My life's motivators

As I moved forward, I carried with me the lessons learned from diverse experiences, ready to apply them to my own aspirations and journey of becoming. But how did I get where I was?

Dreams; those ambitions that flickered on the edge of attainability. What if we could have everything we ever desired — not what we thought we could get, but the limitless expanse of possibilities?

This question often ignited spirited conversations among friends, each voicing desires that sent our imaginations flying. Think about kids when they go wild with their wishes, dreaming of lives filled with adventure; a personal chef who conjured culinary wonders, and a portfolio of properties to rival a real estate VIP.

Is it just fantasy? I would say, it highlights the human spirit's boundless aspiration. Conversations with my friends often ventured into the domain of ambition and career. Some of us set our sights on aspirations that others dismissed as unattainable. The doubters and naysayers were numerous, their words as heavy as boulders. Some friends said, "You'll never achieve that. It's out of your league." But that only fueled my determination. I couldn't wait to ride on the waves of success and say, with a knowing smile, "Oh, sorry, you were wrong."

One time with friends, during my university years, we were discussing our dreams and plans. I shared my dream of one day working in Silicon Valley, an ambition that seemed almost unattainable from where I sat at that time. My friends looked at me with skepticism. "That's a big dream," one said. "Maybe too big." But in my heart, I knew it was more than a wild fantasy. I learned that dreams push us to cultivate the qualities and skills necessary to make a meaningful impact in our chosen fields.

I've come to understand that it's not merely the attainment of things that defines our worth, but the person we become in pursuit of these aspirations; nurturing the qualities and skills that make us attractive to the marketplace or to the world of business. By chasing dreams, we're becoming the influences we aspire to wield.

I also learned how important it is to take care of ourselves. Throughout my journey, I discovered that prioritizing self-care was not indulgence but rather a potent tool for personal growth and development.

At its core, self-care involves nurturing one's physical, emotional, and mental well-being, recognizing that in order to become the influence we aspire to be, we must first take care of ourselves.

Incorporating self-care into my daily routine transformed my approach to self-improvement. It shifted my perspective from merely chasing external achievements to recognizing that taking care of myself was an essential part of the journey. It's like the advice we receive on an airplane. They don't advise you to secure your child's mask first. They say, "Put your mask on first before assisting others." Taking care of yourself is paramount before you can effectively care for others.

I remember finding myself in my apartment, lying on the bed, exhausted and depleted. It was a wake-up call. I understood then that neglecting my well-being was not sustainable and was counterproductive to my aspirations. This led me to gradually introduce self-care practices into my daily life.

I started with small changes: ensuring I ate nutritious meals, setting aside time for exercise, and most importantly, allowing myself moments of rest and relaxation.

Over time, these practices became part of my routine, fundamentally changing how I approached my personal and professional life. I noticed significant improvement in my focus, creativity, and overall happiness, refusing to make excuses. Those cunning deceivers that often manifest in various forms — "No, I cannot. This car costs too much." No, it doesn't cost too much. You simply can't afford it.

Something to keep in mind is that success isn't only about professional achievements but also about maintaining a healthy balance in life.

On a personal note, I had to learn the importance of punctuality the hard way. There was a period when I would often arrive late for meetings. It seemed trivial to me until I missed a crucial job interview because of my tardiness. That experience taught me a valuable lesson. Being on time is a sign of respect and is appreciated universally.

While some people might be forgiving of lateness, for others, it's a deal-breaker. A lost opportunity, especially one that could have been avoided with punctuality, can be a hard lesson.

This concept extends to how we nourish our minds as well. Think of your mind as something that needs regular feeding, just like your body. Of course, physical food is important, but so is intellectual nourishment.

Pessimism, with its clouded vision, tries to make you see the negative side. They say the glass is half full. But it's also half empty.

Manage it! The key is to educate the pessimism within you. Learn from experiences, even the ones that didn't go as planned.

Reflecting on this, after I graduated, I went through numerous job interviews, each time facing rejection. Those interviews could easily have been seen as failures, but I chose to view them as opportunities to refine my approach.

Each interview that didn't result in a job offer was a learning experience. Maybe I stumbled over a technical question, or perhaps I didn't express my ideas clearly enough. Rather than letting these experiences dishearten me, I used them to improve.

I practiced my responses, honed my technical knowledge, and worked on presenting my thoughts more coherently. This habit enriched my mind and expanded my perspective in ways I never expected. I often said that reading a good book was like giving my brain a hearty meal, full of nutrients and energy.

I often think about life as the seasons change. Changes in seasons are relentless, and with them, the cycles of life and business continue. We witness the ebb and flow of success and recession; learning to navigate these transitions is essential. Just like you can't skip January by tearing off a calendar page, we can't avoid life's challenges by wishing them away.

Instead of hoping for an easier path, it's wiser to strive to become better ourselves. Yearning for fewer challenges is futile; what we need is more wisdom and skills to tackle them. Spring, often cold and harsh, represents the opportunity that follows the winter of our struggles. Just as surely as day follows night, we must be prepared for change.

Like the seasons, what happens to us is common, part of the human experience. It's our actions in response that make the difference. If we don't change our approach, our future will mirror our past. Look back at the last five years — if you desire a different outcome, it's time for a change.

Even if it's uncomfortable or unappealing, learning and gathering information is crucial.

When you have strong reasons — whether for recognition, respect, or family — you can achieve incredible things. We often underestimate our own intelligence; we are capable of a lot more than what our current situations might suggest.

The future isn't shaped by hopes, but by plans and actions. I learned this when I decided to stop being overly cautious and take a chance. If you've survived everything up to this point, instead of dwelling on the negative or what went wrong, focus on how you can succeed by starting to do the right things now.

Confidence begins with awareness. Both life and business are about adapting to changing seasons, and the real challenge lies in understanding how to handle these changes.

The future isn't shaped by hopes, but by plans and actions. This statement resonates deeply with me, especially when I recall an experience from my professional life.

There was a director at one of the companies I worked for who had a particularly pragmatic approach to business. Whenever someone in the team would say something like, "I hope we can complete the task today," he would loudly respond with dry humor: "Hope? This is not a church."

His point was clear: concrete plans and decisive actions are what drive results and progress, not just wishful thinking.

I realize how this approach has shaped my perspective. It taught me the importance of transforming hopes into actionable plans. For instance, hoping to meet a deadline is vastly different from creating a detailed plan, assigning specific tasks, and actively tracking progress to ensure the deadline is met.

This experience also highlighted the value of being proactive rather than reactive. In a business setting, and even in personal goals, a proactive stance involves anticipating challenges, preparing for them, and taking steps to mitigate them before they become obstacles, creating strategies and contingency plans, rather than just hoping things will work out.

I learned that while hope can be a source of motivation, it is the combination of well-thought-out plans and committed actions that truly shape the future. This lesson has been invaluable in my career and personal life. Reinforcing that success is a product of planning and doing, not just wishing and hoping.

When progressing on our journeys, there will always be concerns that might turn into worries to avoid, and even fears. The key is to face the facts, make decisions, and balance them with faith. Faith is something you develop, while facts are what you learn and understand. We need to see things as they are, but also better than they are, to be inspired to act.

Read as much as you can. Focus on books that will make you unique, productive, and wealthy. Knowledge is a key ingredient in navigating life's seasons and making the most of every opportunity that comes your way.

Another factor that shaped my life is learning from negative experiences. It teaches us what not to do. There was a period in my life that became a case study in the consequences of poor choices. It underscored the importance of patience, hard work, and making decisions that are not just beneficial in the short term but sustainable in the long run.

As I discussed in previous chapters, in my hometown, people my age (I was twenty-two) were falling into the trap of illegal activities. These experiences served as a powerful lesson, emphasizing the importance of thorough understanding and learning to avoid repeating such mistakes, especially if one's goal is to achieve success.

In my journey, I've learned a crucial lesson: You don't need everything around you to be perfect to find success. It's not about having a booming economy, the perfect soil for planting, or consistent sunshine and rain.

What really matters is making the best of what you have. At times, it can be tempting to blame external factors for our challenges — the school system, teachers, the company we work for, its policies, the marketplace, even the government. But what happens when you run out of things to blame?

I remember a time in my life when I was caught in this cycle of blame. It seemed easier to point fingers at everything around me rather than looking inward. But this mindset was a trap, one that led to stagnation rather than growth. I realized that blaming the tools and conditions at my disposal was a mistake. It was a failure to recognize that these elements were all I had to work with.

As I progressed in my personal and professional life, I understood that if I wanted different results, I couldn't rely on changing the external environment — the seed, the soil, the weather. These were beyond my control. The real change had to come from within. It was about shifting my philosophy, my way of thinking, my entire approach to life and work.

Once I started focusing on improving myself, changing my attitude, and enhancing my skills, things began to shift. I learned to work with what I had, to adapt and make the most of any situation. This change in mindset turned out to be the key to unlocking doors I previously thought were closed.

It wasn't the external factors that needed to change; it was me. This realization has been a guiding principle in my journey, helping me navigate various challenges and seize opportunities I once thought were out of reach.

The idea that you can achieve more than you currently have by becoming more than you currently are, is a powerful concept. It's rooted in the belief that personal growth and development are the keys to unlocking greater success and prosperity. This holds particularly true when it comes to income.

While your income might occasionally take a lucky leap forward, it won't sustainably stay there unless your personal development keeps pace. In essence, your income rarely, if ever, exceeds your personal growth.

Consider this: If someone suddenly hands you a million dollars, you're faced with a big challenge. To keep and grow this wealth, you need to give yourself the mindset and capabilities of a millionaire, perhaps even a billionaire, quickly adapting to a new level of thinking, decision-making, and responsibility.

If you fail to grow into your new financial status, it's likely the money will slip through your fingers, returning you to where you were before. I always thought this was why the richest are few.

In my own life, this principle has been a guiding force. I've realized that in order to achieve and maintain certain levels of success, I need to continuously invest in my personal growth and development. This applies to financial matters and to all areas of life. Expanding my knowledge, improving my skills, and feeding my mind are all critical components of this growth, of continuously evolving and adapting to new circumstances and higher levels of achievement.

The journey of personal growth is ongoing; it doesn't have a final destination. Each new level of success and every increase in income should be matched by a corresponding increase in personal development. This balance ensures that you reach new heights and have the capacity to sustain and build upon them. This philosophy has been instrumental in my progress and has helped me achieve more than I had and become more than I was.

Another concept I tried to wrap my head around is that the things easy to do are also easy to ignore. Every day, we're faced with choices to do the easy tasks or to overlook them. I learned that neglecting these small, easy actions can start harmlessly but grow into a significant problem, much like an infection that turns into a disease if left untreated.

Neglect and inaction can set you on a path you never intended to follow, leading you to become someone you never wanted to be, living a life you never desired.

This principle became clear to me as I observed the patterns of failure and success around me, starting from my hometown, ending in

Silicon Valley. Failure often stems from making small, poor decisions consistently over time. Daily errors in judgment, while seemingly insignificant at the time, accumulate and lead to long-term problems.

Consider the approach to finances as an example. Many people who struggle financially spend their money first and then think about saving or investing whatever little might be left. On the other hand, those who achieve financial stability and wealth typically do the opposite. They prioritize investing their money and then spend what remains. This habit, easy to implement but also easy to neglect, makes a significant difference in one's financial health.

In my journey, I've learned the importance of not overlooking the small, easy actions. Whether it's making smart financial decisions, investing in personal growth, or just handling daily responsibilities, the cumulative effect of these choices defines the trajectory of our lives. By choosing to do what is easy to do, rather than neglecting it, we set ourselves on a path to success and fulfillment, avoiding the pitfalls of becoming what we never wanted to be.

My understanding of the importance of wise financial habits was shaped by a personal experience early in my career. After receiving my first significant paycheck, I was tempted to spend it on immediate gratifications — a new gadget, expensive dinners, and designer Italian clothes. It seemed natural to reward myself for the hard work.

A conversation with a colleague changed my perspective.

One day, over lunch, this colleague, who I admired for his financial savvy, shared his approach to money. He spoke about how he prioritized saving and investing a portion of his income before spending on non-essentials. The strategy was simple yet effective: pay yourself first, then live within the means of what's left.

Intrigued, I started setting aside a portion of my paycheck for savings and investments, treating it as a non-negotiable expense, just like rent or utilities. Of course, It wasn't always easy, especially when tempted by short-term pleasures, but I remained disciplined.

This small shift in my financial habits brought about significant changes. I was able to build a safety net, invest in opportunities that came my way, and enjoy a sense of security and peace of mind I hadn't known before.

This practice also spilled over into other areas of my life. I began to see the value in small, consistent actions, whether it was in maintaining personal relationships, pursuing professional development, or managing day-to-day responsibilities.

Your philosophy, the way you view and approach life, inevitably determines where you end up. I often pause and reflect on the past six years, thinking of my mistakes. I learned that correcting those mistakes ensures bigger fruits in the next six years.

Even if it seems like you don't need to make changes, if there's even a slight chance you do, start planning those changes in the next two years. This period represents a golden opportunity to transform your income, your future, and your life. Humans have the remarkable ability to change their life trajectory.

You're not bound to repeat the patterns of your past six years. You, my friend, enemy, or person in my little hometown — you have the power to significantly alter the course of your life.

Consider this: Five years from now, you will arrive somewhere. The critical question is, where will that be?

This is a serious matter. If you continue with your current discipline and the path you've been following, where will you find yourself in five years? Without deliberate planning, you might end up in a place you never intended to be, wearing clothes you don't like, driving a car you don't enjoy, living in a place you don't want to live, or even doing a job you despise. All of this can happen simply because you didn't consciously design a better destination for yourself.

I hope that you aim for a well-planned and fulfilling destination; a place where you are productive, respected, and honored; a place that makes you feel good about yourself and gives you the influence to positively impact others in ways you can't imagine today. Remember, we move in the direction we face. If you start designing your future now, you'll begin moving towards it.

I found it crucial to continually challenge and exercise my mind. Engage in debates, read extensively, and understand both sides of every argument. Don't exclude yourself from important conversations and big debates of our time. Be in that room.

Consistency led me to predictable outcomes. If you do something often enough, a pattern or ratio will emerge. This can be applied to habits, efforts in work, or even personal development. Recognizing and understanding these ratios in different aspects of your life can help you make better informed decisions and guide you toward your well-designed future.

Conclusion

As my journey from the humble streets of Calabria to the innovative landscape of Silicon Valley comes to a close in these pages, I reflect on the incredible journey I've embarked upon. It's a story that began as a simple dream in a small town, nurtured by the values and love of my humble parents and the lively company of my four younger brothers.

Each step of my path, from the scenic shores of South Italy to the bustling heart of the tech world, represented the power of ambition, hard work, and the importance of holding onto one's roots.

Throughout this journey, my life has been a blend of embracing the new while cherishing the old. The lessons learned in the warmth of my family home in the South of Italy have been my guiding star, even as I navigated the unknown territories of technology and innovation in the United States. My story shows that no matter how far we travel or how much we achieve, our origins and the values instilled in us play a crucial role in shaping our lives.

As I look back, I realize that the dreams of a young boy from Calabria have not only been fulfilled but have also paved the way for new aspirations. This story, which spans continents and cultures, is a testament to the fact that with determination and a willingness to learn, it's possible to transcend boundaries and achieve what once seemed impossible.

I hope my story inspires others to dream big and work tirelessly towards those dreams, regardless of where they start. May it serve as an encouragement that with perseverance, a strong sense of self, and a dash of courage, one can navigate through life's challenges and embrace the opportunities that come along.

I've encountered numerous challenges, each teaching me invaluable lessons. There were moments of doubt and struggle, like the early days in Silicon Valley, where I grappled with a new culture and work environment. Overcoming these hurdles shaped and strengthened my resilience. For instance, adjusting to the fast-paced tech world while maintaining my well-being was a balancing act that took time to master. These experiences were crucial, reinforcing the idea that success is not just about reaching a destination, but also about overcoming the obstacles along the way.

Looking ahead, my journey doesn't end here. The future holds new challenges and opportunities, and my goal is to continue growing, learning, and contributing to both my field and community. Whether it's mentoring young professionals or exploring new technological frontiers, I am excited about what lies ahead.

This story, a blend of past achievements and future aspirations, is a shared gift to you that showcases how our life journey is ever-evolving. Just as my roots in Calabria grounded me, my experiences in Silicon Valley propel me forward, driving me to reach new heights and explore uncharted territories.

In closing, I carry with me the memories and experiences of my journey and the enduring spirit of Calabria. This is who I am and where I come from. This journey helped me discover myself, push boundaries, and find success in unexpected places. Always remember that our beginnings, no matter how modest, can lead to extraordinary destinations.